Contents

Shiny materials

Some things are shiny.

Properties of Materials

Shiny or Dull

Charlotte Guillain

www.raintreepublishers.co.uk
Visit our website to find out more information about Raintree books.

To order:
☎ Phone 0845 6044371
🖷 Fax +44 (0) 1865 312263
✉ Email myorders@capstonepub.co.uk

Customers from outside the UK please telephone +44 1865 312262

Raintree is an imprint of Capstone Global Library Limited, a company incorporated in England and Wales having its registered office at 7 Pilgrim Street, London, EC4V 6LB – Registered company number: 6695582

"Raintree" is a registered trademark of Pearson Education Limited, under licence to Capstone Global Library Limited

Text © Capstone Global Library Limited
First published in hardback in 2009
Paperback edition first published in 2010
The moral rights of the proprietor have been asserted.

Edited by Charlotte Guillain and Catherine Veitch
Designed by Joanna Hinton-Malivoire
Picture research by Elizabeth Alexander
Originated by Heinemann Library
Printed by South China Printing Company Limited

ISBN 978 0 431 19348 9 (hardback)
13 12 11 10 09
10 9 8 7 6 5 4 3 2 1

ISBN 978 0 431 19356 4 (paperback)
14 13 12 11 10
10 9 8 7 6 5 4 3 2 1

British Library Cataloguing in Publication Data
Guillain, Charlotte
Shiny or dull. - (Properties of materials)
530.4
A full catalogue record for this book is available from the British Library.

Acknowledgements
The author and publishers are grateful to the following for permission to reproduce copyright material:
Alamy p. **18** (© foodfolio); © Capstone Publishers p. **22** (Karon Dubke); Corbis pp. **5** (© Fancy/Veer), **20** (© Frithjof Hirdes/zefa); Getty Images p. 8 (Gavin Hellier/Robert Harding); Photolibrary pp. **9** (Frazer Cunningham/Mode Images), **11** (Corbis), **13** (Yves Regaldi/Zen Shui), **15** (Creatas/Comstock), **16, 23** top (Chuck Pefley/Tips Italia), **19** (Yoav Levy/Phototake Science); Shutterstock pp. **4** (© Christopher Elwell), **6** (© garloon), **7, 23** bottom (© Sailorr), **10** (© Rafal Olechowski), **12** (© Tony Sanchez-Espinosa), **14, 23** middle (© Mike Flippo), **17** (© Marie C. Fields), **21** (© OkapiStudio).

Cover photograph of skyscrapers reproduced with permission of Shutterstock (© Serp). Back cover photograph of a yoyo reproduced with permission of Shutterstock (© Mike Flippo).

The publishers would like to thank Nancy Harris and Adriana Scalise for their assistance in the preparation of this book.

Shiny things can be smooth.

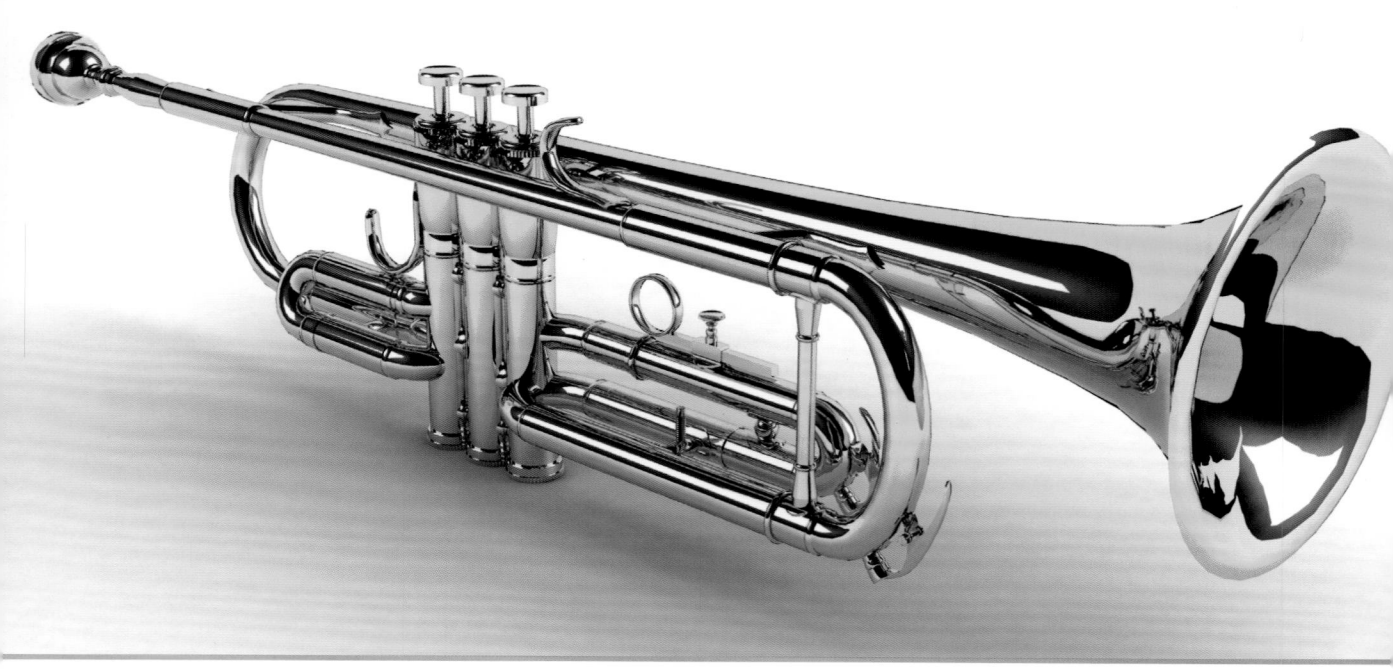

Shiny things can be hard.

Light makes shiny things shine a lot.

Dull materials

Some things are dull.

rough

smooth

Dull things can be smooth or rough.

Dull things can be hard or soft.

Light makes dull things shine a little.

Shiny and dull materials

Rock can be shiny. It can be smooth.
It can be hard.

Rock can be dull.

It can be rough. It can be hard.

Plastic can be shiny.

It can be smooth. It can be hard.

Cotton can be dull.
It can be rough. It can be soft.

Metal can be shiny.

It can be smooth. It can be hard.

Paper can be dull.
It can be smooth. It can be soft.

You cannot feel if something is shiny or dull.

shiny

You can see if something is shiny or dull.

You can see a shiny thing is smooth.

You can see a dull thing is rough.

Quiz

Which of these things are shiny?
Which of these things are dull?

Picture glossary

 **metal** hard, shiny material

 **plastic** material that can be soft or hard

 **shiny** bright. Shiny things reflect light.

Index

Note to parents and teachers
Before reading
Tell children that you can see if an object is shiny or dull. Shiny things can be smooth; they can be hard, and light makes shiny things shine a lot. Dull things are not shiny; they can be smooth, hard, and light makes dull things shine only a little. Show children pictures of shiny and dull materials. Let children guess and explain why some of the materials in the pictures are shiny or dull.

After reading
Give children a bag of objects. They are to take the objects and decide if they are shiny or dull. Ask children to feel the objects and decide if they are hard or soft, or rough or smooth. When the children have finished sorting, get them to turn and talk to a partner. Ask them to discuss the objects. Ask children: "Did you and your partner sort the objects in the same way?", "What do your objects have in common?", "How are they different?".